AMAZING, MISUNDERSTOOD BATS

Marta Magellan

Big Brown Bat

Eifrig Publishing LLC

Berlin Lemont

Dedicated in loving memory of Sammy Joe Schnall

Manuscript vetted by Marcia Daniels and the Merlin Tuttle Organization.

Thank You to Ruth Vander Zee, Silvia Lopez, and the SCBWI Coral Gables Picture Book Group for their generous help critiquing the manuscript.

Special Thanks to Cathy Snyder, Anne Crawford, Marilyn Smith, and Penny Eifrig, whose encouraging support has made this book possible

Cover and book design by Tamian Wood
www.BeyondDesignInternational.com

Published by Eifrig Publishing,
PO Box 66, Lemont, PA 16851, USA
Knobelsdorffstr. 44, 14059 Berlin, Germany.
For information regarding permission, write to:
Rights and Permissions Department,
Eifrig Publishing,
PO Box 66, Lemont, PA 16851, USA.
permissions@eifrigpublishing.com, +1-888-340-6543

Library of Congress Cataloging-in-Publication Data
  Magellan, Marta
Amazing, Misunderstood Bats/
by Marta Magellan
p. cm.

Paperback: ISBN 978-1-63233-211-0
Hardcover: ISBN 978-1-63233-213-4
eBook: ISBN 978-1-63233-212-7
[1. Nature - Juvenile Nonfiction. 2. Animals - Bats, Mammals, Pollinators - Juvenile Nonfiction

I. Magellan, Mauro, ill. II. Title
23 22 21 20 2019
5 4 3 2 1

Printed on recycled PCW acid-free paper.

THE MISUNDERSTOOD BUT AMAZING BAT

Maybe you don't like bats. But if you don't, you will want to adjust your bat attitude once you read about these amazing creatures. They are probably the most misunderstood of all animals.

They hang upside down in dark places, only go out at night, and fly high up in the dark skies with their eerie, pointy wings. True. They've also been known to suck blood and turn into evil vampires. Not so true.

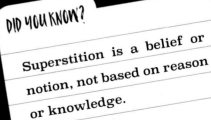

Hoary Bat

Some of those misunderstandings are superstitions. Others are just plain wrong. Bats are amazing animals. They help clear the world of bugs, pollinate plants, grow forests, and much more.

DID YOU KNOW?

Superstition is a belief or notion, not based on reason or knowledge.

BATS POLLINATE PLANTS

Bats do something super important. They help plants grow. Plants can't travel, so they depend on animals to take pollen from one plant or part of a plant to another. That way, new plant seeds can be made. Bats go into a flower to sip nectar, and the pollen sticks to their fur. Even bats that eat insects sometimes follow the bugs into flowers, then carry the pollen out. Bats, not birds or bees, are the world's best long-distance pollinator. There are over 500 plants that rely on the help of bats. If you like bananas or chocolates, thank a bat.

SOMETHING TO LEARN

Pollen is a fine powdery substance, typically yellow, consisting of microscopic grains necessary for producing seeds. Wind, insects, bats and other animals carry pollen from one part of a flower to the other.

5

BATS HELP KEEP FORESTS GROWING

There are hundreds of species of bats that make rainforests grow and deserts bloom. These bats eat the fruit and the seed of many plants. Then, they poop the seeds out all over as they fly. The seeds grow into trees in the forests. Lush forests are good for people and animals all over the world, no matter where they live.

Cuban fruit-eating bat

Jamaican fruit-eating bat

Big Brown Bat eating a moth in flight

BATS GOBBLE UP BUGS

Some people think bats are pests – not so! Bats eat pests. They gobble up loads of insects that damage crops and gardens. They also eat insects that cause disease in humans. Some bats can eat as many as 1,000 bugs in ONE hour. Most of us wouldn't mind if those were all mosquitoes. But bats eat all kinds of bugs and keep them under control. Imagine how much bug spray we'd have to use if there weren't any bats.

FUN FACT

At dusk over 400,000 hungry bats fly out of two bat houses (more like bat hotels) on the University of Florida campus in Gainesville, Florida. What do they do? They eat pesky insects. Yay!

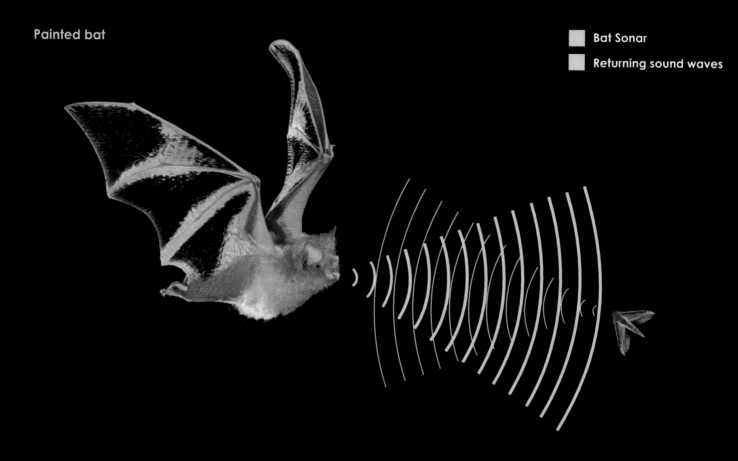

Painted bat

BATS CAN "SEE" WITH SOUND

Bats have a sure-fire way to catch even tiny bugs while flying through the air. It's called echolocation, and it's the way they can hunt in the inky blackness of night. They locate the bugs by emitting a high-pitched sound that bounces off the insect to the bat's ears. From this echo the bat can tell where the bug or object is.

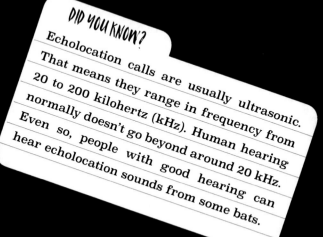

FUN BAT FACTS!

Bats make sounds for echolocation the same way people make sounds when they talk or sing. Both move air past their vibrating vocal chords. Some bats emit the sounds from their mouth. Others emit sound through their nose.

DID YOU KNOW?

Echolocation calls are usually ultrasonic. That means they range in frequency from 20 to 200 kilohertz (kHz). Human hearing normally doesn't go beyond around 20 kHz. Even so, people with good hearing can hear echolocation sounds from some bats.

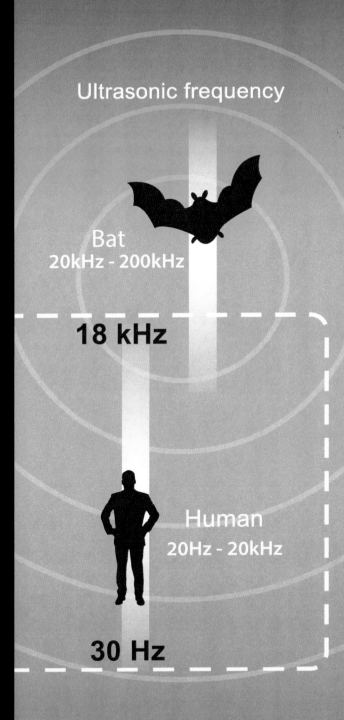

Ultrasonic frequency

Bat
20kHz - 200kHz

18 kHz

Human
20Hz - 20kHz

30 Hz

Eastern red bat

INCREDIBLE BUT TRUE!

Robotic engineers have developed a flying robot by studying bat wings. Called the Bat Bot, it can fly, turn and swoop like a bat. These bat robots will be able to help inspect disaster zones, fly into tight crawl spaces, such as mines or collapsed buildings, and maybe fetch things for elderly people.

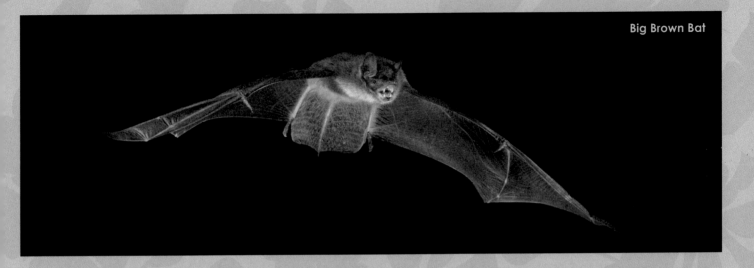

Big Brown Bat

BATS ARE THE ONLY MAMMALS THAT CAN FLY

Some mammals can glide, like the flying squirrel, but bats are the only mammal that can truly fly. The scientific name for bats, Chiroptera (ky-ROP-ter-a), means "hand wing." That's because the bat's hand is also its wing. Bats have arms, elbows, and four fingers and a thumb -- just like people. The fingers are almost as long as the rest of the body. Bats are super-good flyers, maybe better than birds!

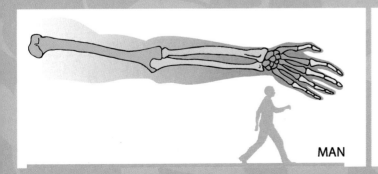

MAN

BAT

BATS HELP FERTILIZE CROPS

Fertilizer is a natural or chemical mixture that you spread on the ground in order to make plants grow better. The word for bat poop is **guano,** and it is used as a fertilizer. It has helped farmers for thousands of years. Guano is rich in three important nutrients (nourishment) for plants. Big farms use chemical **fertilizers** now, but many organic farmers today still use bat guano for their crops.

SOMETHING TO LEARN

Nitrogen, phosphorus and potassium, or NPK, are the most important **nutrients** in fertilizers. Each of these **nutrients** plays a role in helping plants grow. Nitrogen is considered to be the most important one because plants absorb more nitrogen than anything else.

14

BATS HELP MEDICAL SCIENCE

common vampire bat

The vampire bat, exaggerated as being a dangerous killer, is the one that may help medical doctors. Blood **clots** (clumps of dried blood) tend to be dangerous. A clot can go to the patient's brain. Bat **saliva** (spit) has something in it that keeps the blood from clotting. It is a hundred times more powerful than drugs made to get rid of clots. The chemical in vampire bat saliva tackles just the clot and doesn't interfere with anything else in the blood. Real vampire bats may someday save many lives...more than the scary fake ones kill in horror movies!

NEW BAT WORD:
The clot-dissolving chemical in vampire bat saliva has a long four-word name, but is better known as Desmotoplase.

15

THE MISUNDERSTOOD BAT

Bats are the most misunderstood of all mammals. Many people are afraid of them. They are considered spooky and associated with Halloween and vampires. There are those who even believe they will fly into your hair (they won't – echolocation, you know).

DID YOU KNOW?
Vampire bats are small bats that feed on the blood of cows, deer, horses, and birds, found mainly in Latin America.

BATS ARE **NOT** BLOOD SUCKERS

No bats will probably ever bite you to suck your blood. There are over 1,300 species of bats in the world, but only three of them like the taste of blood. They are called vampire bats and they live in Mexico and South America. Vampire bats prefer to pierce the skin of an animal, like a chicken or a cow, and lap the blood up with their tongues. It's like a mosquito bite to them.

No sucking involved.

vampire bat

Mammals are animals that nurse their young, have hair or fur, and are warm-blooded.

BATS ARE NOT FLYING MICE OR RATS

Rats rhymes with bats, and they are both mammals. But that's about it. If you look closely at the faces of bats, you'll see they look very different from rats. Also, they don't behave like rats. Bats don't chew on things like wood, metal, or your plastic bag of potato chips. Scientists have placed bats in a group all their own called **Chiroptera** (ky-ROP-ter-a).

NEW BAT WORD:

Chiroptera: The scientific name for bats. It means "hand wing."

BATS ARE NOT BLIND

If you ever heard someone say "blind as a bat," it's definitely not true. They don't have the sharp and colorful visions humans have, but at **dawn** and **dusk**, they see better than we do. Some bats, like fruit bats, hunt using sight alone. They have large eyes and binocular vision.

Even the small insect-eating bats with poorer eyesight rely on visual clues to navigate long distances.

WORDS TO LEARN

Dawn the first appearance of light in the sky before sunrise.

Dusk the darkest stage after sunset and just before night.

DID YOU KNOW?

Navigate means to carefully travel over long stretches of land or water.

21

BATS ARE NOT ALL DISEASED WITH RABIES

Bats do get **rabies** but much less often than other mammals. Raccoons, foxes, even dogs are much more likely to bite a human and pass on rabies. Bats become paralyzed when they get rabies and can't fly. They can't even hang on long enough to **roost**. So stay away from bats on the ground. That way, you're not going to get rabies. Whew. Isn't that a relief? Except that now you'll be extra careful around raccoons and stray dogs. And that's smart.

DID YOU KNOW?

Rabies is a dangerous disease from a virus that can be passed on to humans by sick mammals. The Center for Disease Control states: "Love your own, leave other animals alone" to avoid being bit.

22

Healthy Brazilian free-tailed bats, roosting

FUN FACT:
When bats roost, they are resting in the place where they take a break from flying. Bats roosting upside down or flying are usually in good health.

Brazilian free-tailed bats emerging from cave

BATS ARE FUN!

Watching bats emerge from their caves and houses is exciting. It is a big event in Austin, Texas and Gainesville, Florida, as well as other places where bats live. People wait at dusk to see huge numbers of bats emerge from their roosting places and even from bat houses built just for them. Now you have to

MORE FACTS ABOUT BATS

Habitats: Bats are losing their habitats. This means they don't have the same number of caves and forests to roost in as in the past. People have started to build bat houses for them. Bats now roost by the thousands in special places built just for them, like the ones in Gainesville Florida.

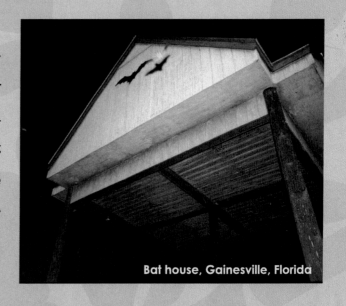
Bat house, Gainesville, Florida

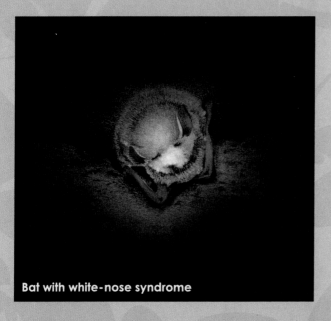
Bat with white-nose syndrome

White-nose syndrome: Millions of bats have died of a disease in the United States and Canada. White nose syndrome is caused by a fungus that grows in cold and humid environments, such as bat caves. We can best help bats by protecting their habitats and leaving them alone.

25

Bat feet: A bat's feet makes them able to grasp objects like twigs and branches. Sharp claws in their feet hook into cracks in the wall or ceilings of a cave. These claws are so strong that they support the bat's whole weight, even during sleep. That's because they have a locking ability that allows them to hang freely without having to exert any energy.

ABOUT BATS

There are over 1,300 species throughout the world. Florida alone has 13 native species of bats, though at least 20 species have been found in the state, such as the Cuban flower bat, the Cuban fruit bat, the Jamaican fruit bat, and other non-natives. Some are common across the state, while some live in only a small area or migrate there for part of the year.

Rafinesque's big-eared bats

BATS IN FLORIDA

1. Brazilian free-tailed bat
2. Southeastern myotis
3. Evening bat
4. Eastern red bat
5. Seminole bat
6. Northern yellow bat
7. Tricolored bat
8. Big brown bat
9. Rafinesque's big-eared bat
10. Hoary bat
11. Velvety free-tailed bat
12. Florida bonneted bat ENDANGERED
13. Gray bat ENDANGERED

GLOSSARY

Chiroptera the scientific name for bats, meaning "hand wing"

Clots thick and sticky clumps of dried blood that stops the regular flow through a blood vessel

Dawn the first appearance of light in the sky before sunrise

Desmotoplase the chemical in bat saliva that dissolves clots

Dusk the darkest stage after sunset and just before night

Echolocation determining the location of something like a flying bug by measuring the time it takes for an echo to return from it

Fertilizers a substance that is added to the soil to help plants grow

Guano bat poop

Habitat the home of an animal, including the plants, water, soil and air around it

Mammals animals that nurse their young, have hair or fur, and are warm-blooded

Navigate to travel over long stretches of land or water

Pollen a fine powdery substance, typically yellow, consisting of microscopic grains necessary for producing seeds. Wind, insects, bats and other animals carry pollen from one part of a flower to the other

Pollinate to transfer pollen from the male part of the plant to the female part to make seedlings, which become new plants

Rabies a dangerous disease from a virus that can be passed on to humans from mammals such as raccoons

Roost the place where bats and certain types of birds take a break from flying

Saliva formal word for spit

Superstition a belief or notion, not based on reason or knowledge

Vampire bat a small bat that feeds on the blood of cows, deer, horses, and birds, found mainly in Latin America

White nose syndrome a fungus that lives in cold and humid areas like caves, causing diseased bats to die

ABOUT THE AUTHOR

Marta Magellan's interest in children, literacy, and nature has produced many published nonfiction books on animals for children. She has written about lizards, big cats, vultures, and Burmese pythons. She has also written children's books for the educational market and travel articles on exotic places. Her life and career have always revolved around writing. She taught Composition, Creative Writing, and Survey of Children's Literature, at Miami Dade College, where she was a full professor and adviser to an award-winning literary arts magazine. Visit her at www.martamagellan.com.

PHOTO AND ILLUSTRATION CREDITS

All photos by Merlin Tuttle of MerlinTuttle.org except:
Pages 12 and 13 Eastern Red Bat and Big Brown Bat photos by Brock Fenton
Page 25 illustration of bat with white-nose syndrome by Mauro Magellan
Page 26 bat feet from Depositphotos.com
Book Design by Tamian Wood, BeyondDesignInternational.com
Cover illustration by Mauro Magellan

Want to learn more about bats? Check out Merlin Tuttle's Bat Conservation site at www.merlintuttle.org

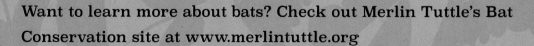

SELECTED REFERENCES

Cosgrove, Ben. (12 Aug. 2012). Why bats are so misunderstood. *Time*.
http://ideas.time.com/2012/08/10/why-bats-ar-so-misunderstood/

Florida Museum. (8 Feb. 2018) Five Facts about Bats in Florida.
https://www.floridamuseum.ufl.edu/science/five-facts-bats-in-florida/

Marks, Cynthia S. and George E. Marks. (2006). *Bats of Florida*. University
Press of Florida. Gainesville. Print.

Harris, Tom. (1 June 2001, Date of Access 7 November 2018). How Bats Work.
HowStuffWorks. https://animals.howstuffworks.com/

Henderstrom, A. and L. Christoffer Johanssen. (18 May 2015). Bat flight. *Current
Science*. 18 Volume 25, Issue 10. Pages R399-R402.
https://doi.org/10.1016/j.cub.2015.04.002

Ramezani, A., Soon-Jo Chung, Seth Hutchinson. (01 Feb. 2017). A biomimetic
robotic platform to study flight specializations of bats. Science Robotics.
Vol. 2, Issue 3, eaal2505 DOI: 10.1126/scirobotics.aal2505

Read, Merrill. (18 June 2018). Bats love to pollinate. *The Echo*.
http://www.batcon.org/resources/media-education/news-room/
the-echo/1184-pollinator-week

U.S. Forest Service. Date of Access: (20 Sept. 2018). Bats. *United States Department
of Agriculture*. https://www.fs.fed.us/visit/know-before-you-go/bats

INDEX

(Numbers in *italics* refer to photographs)

17204132R00020